VEGAN FOIL PACKET COOKBOOK:

Top 30 Vegan Recipes - Using Foil Packets For Grilling Vegetables!

By

KATYA JOHANSSON

Table of Contents

INTRODUCTION

Wrapping foods in individual foil packets allows them to steam-cook to perfection and let the flavors blend well.

They are so easy to make and you can easily customize them per person. Foil also keeps your fresh veggies from touching whatever dirtiness is nearby, especially when camping.

Packets can be cooked in an oven or on a grill on medium-high. Each packet acts as both main and side dish and they are so easy to put together.

The best way to do this is getting them together the night before, so that the flavors meld together more and you have them ready the next day.

Chopped vegetables wrapped in tinfoil and roasted are best when you also mix in seitan or tofu. An excellent possibility is to make kabobs from seitan or tofu. You can also include some protein in there by marinating tempeh in in any marinade of your choice and arrange it in, with the veggies before putting them on the grill.

How to make foil packs?

1. Lay a large sheet of heavy-duty foil or a double layer of regular foil on a flat surface.

2. Cut squares of parchment paper and put them on top of aluminum foil, if you want the tight fit of the foil but don't want the foil touching the food.

3. Put the ingredients in the center of the parchment paper and foil.

4. Bring the short ends of the foil together and fold twice to seal; fold in the sides to seal, leaving room for steam.

5. Grill as you like.

GRILLED SEITAN AND SOMMER VEGETABLES

INGREDIENTS:

- 1 seitan package cut in 2 cm. cubes
- 1 large lemon or 2 smaller lemons, thinly sliced
- 2 Tablespoons coconut oil
- 1 zucchini, thinly sliced
- 8 mini bell peppers, sliced (Or 1 regular bell pepper)
- 1 tomato, chopped
- 1 Tablespoon capers, juice drained
- 1 Tablespoon olive oil
- 1 teaspoon sea salt
- ¼ teaspoon black pepper
- Small bunch fresh dill
- Salt
- Pepper
- Cooking spray

METHOD:

1. Preheat the grill to medium high

2. In a bowl, toss together zucchini, bell peppers, tomato, olive oil, salt, and black pepper.

3. Set aside.

4. For each packet, you will need 2 large (about 20 inches long) sheets of foil or just 1 sheet if it's the heavy duty kind.

5. Lay your foil out and spray with cooking spray. (you can brush them with olive oil).

6. Lay one layer of seitan on the foil.

7. Sprinkle with salt and pepper.

8. Place three thin slivers coconut oil on top.

9. Put two slices of lemon on top of the coconut oil.

10. Place a few sprigs of dill on top of that.

11. Place ¼ of the vegetables, including capers beside the other ingredients.

12. Fold the long sides of the foil in towards the center and roll over to seal.

13. Seal up the edges as well.

14. Repeat with remaining ingredients.

15. Place on the preheated grill, cover, and cook for 10-15 minutes.

16. To serve, carefully remove them from the grill and peel back the foil layer.

17. Serve in the foil packet or on plates with the sauce from the bottom of the packet.

GRILLED NEW POTATO PACKET

INGREDIENTS:

- 1 tbsp. Parsley, fresh

- 1/2 lb. Potatoes, red and white new

- 3 tbsp. Kraft sun dried tomato vinaigrette dressing

- 2 tsp. Oil

- 2 tbsp. Tofu cheese, Grated

- 2 tbsp. Water

METHOD:

1. Get it all done on the grill in foil-packet technique.

WILD MUSHROOM AND ASPARAGUS

INGREDIENTS:

- 4 slices whole-grain bread, toasted
- 4 cups thinly sliced wild mushrooms
- 1 lb. thinnest asparagus, cut into 1-inch pieces (3 cups)
- 2 large shallots, thinly sliced (¾ cup)
- 1 ¾ cups low-sodium vegetable broth, divided
- 1 Tbs. minced fresh thyme
- ½ cup crumbled five spice dry tofu cheese

METHOD:

1. Preheat oven to 400°F. Place 4 16-inch lengths of foil on work surface.

2. Fold foil in half from short side. Unfold. Shape corners and edges of one half into semicircular "bowl" with 1/2-inch sides.

3. Coat insides of foil with cooking spray and place 1 slice of toast in each foil packet.

4. Combine mushrooms, asparagus, and shallots in medium bowl. Add 1/4 cup broth, and season with salt and pepper.

5. Divide mixture among packets. Whisk together remaining 1 1/2 cups broth, egg, egg white and thyme in small bowl.

6. Season with salt and pepper, if desired.

7. Drizzle each packet with 1/2 cup broth mixture. Fold other half of foil over ingredients, and crimp edges in overlapping folds until packets are sealed.

8. Transfer packets to baking sheet, and bake 25 to 30 minutes. Transfer to serving plates. Let each person open packet carefully.

9. Sprinkle with crumbled five spice dry tofu cheese

Sweet Potato and Lentil

Ingredients:

- 2 cups finely diced sweet potato
- 1 large red bell pepper, diced (1 ½ cups)
- 1 cup fresh green beans, thinly sliced
- ¼ cup golden raisins
- 2 Tbs. hot sesame oil
- 1 cup low-sodium vegetable broth
- 2 Tbs. minced fresh ginger
- 2 cloves garlic, minced (2 tsp.)
- 1 tsp. curry powder
- 1 ½ cups cooked lentils or 1 15-oz. can lentils, rinsed and drained
- 4 Tbs. prepared mango chutney, optional

Method:

1. Preheat oven to 400°F.
2. Place 4 16-inch lengths of foil on work surface.
3. Fold foil in half from short side. Unfold.

4. Shape corners and edges of one half into semicircular "bowl" with 1/2-inch sides. Coat insides of foil with cooking spray.

5. Combine sweet potato, bell pepper, green beans, and raisins in medium bowl. Add oil, and toss to coat.

6. Season with salt and pepper, if desired.

7. Whisk together broth, ginger, garlic, and curry powder in small bowl. Divide sweet potato mixture among packets; top with 1/3 cup lentils.

8. Pour 1/4 cup broth mixture over lentils, and season with salt and pepper, if desired.

9. Fold other half of foil over ingredients, and crimp edges in overlapping folds until packets are sealed. Transfer packets to baking sheet.

10. Bake 25 minutes.

11. Transfer to plates. Let each person open packet carefully.

12. Escaping air will be hot

13. Top with chutney, if desired.

Vegetable foil packets

Ingredients:

- 1 head broccoli, chopped or 2-3 zucchini, coarsely chopped
- 1/2 medium onion, chopped (this is the best part!)
- 1/3 cup sliced mushrooms
- 1/2 chop snow peas
- 1/2 tsp fresh ginger, minced
- 2 cloves garlic, minced
- 4 tsp olive oil
- 2 tsp sesame oil
- 4 tsp soy sauce

Method:

1. Combine all vegetables, and then divide in half.
2. Place half the vegetables on a large sheet of heavy-duty aluminum foil. Add half of the ginger and half of the garlic to each of the foil packets then drizzle each with half of the olive oil, sesame oil and soy sauce.
3. Wrap foil packets tightly, making sure to seal the edges well so the liquid doesn't escape.

4. Place on the grill for about 10 minutes, poking occasionally to test for doneness, and turning once or twice.

VEGETABLE FOIL PACKET

INGREDIENTS:

- 2 red onions, halved, sliced
- 1 large red bell pepper, seeded, cut into strips
- 1 large zucchini, diced
- 2 broccoli crowns, cut into florets
- 1 (15-ounce) can garbanzo beans, rinsed, drained
- 2 tablespoons minced fresh ginger
- 4 garlic cloves, minced
- Grated zest and juice of 1 lemon
- 1/4 cup finely chopped fresh parsley
- Salt and freshly ground black pepper
- 1/4 cup olive oil

METHOD:

1. Combine all ingredients in a large airtight container, tossing to coat well with the olive oil. Seal and pack.
2. Tear off 4 large sheets of aluminum foil and lay on a flat surface.

3. Toss vegetables well then evenly divide among the sheets of aluminum foil, piling veggies in the center of each sheet.

4. Fold foil over the veg mixture and seal the edges.

5. Set packets in the grill and let cook for 20 minutes or until vegetables are tender.

6. Use tongs to remove packets from the fire. Carefully open packets making sure not to get burned by the steam escaping.

7. Serve immediately.

Hobo Packet

Ingredients:

- Vegan Meaty substitute
- 1/2 a medium onion, thickly sliced
- a handful of baby carrots or 1 large carrot cut into large chunks
- 3 large mushrooms, quartered, or 6 smaller ones halved
- 1 medium sized potato, roughly cubed into about 3/4 to 1 inch pieces
- extra virgin olive oil
- BBQ sauce
- Tamari, soy sauce,
- Hot sauce (optional)
- Salt and pepper

Method:

1. Preheat your oven to 400 degrees Fahrenheit. Get a big piece of aluminum foil, about 18 inches long. Then, smear about a tablespoon of olive oil in the middle, making a puddle big enough to put your fake meat on, about 5 inches in diameter.

2. Put your meat on top of the puddle. Lay your slices of onion on top. Then put the carrots on top of the onions.

At this point, start pinching the sides of the foil together so you've got yourself a little bowl shape. Throw some salt and pepper on at this point, just to season up the aromatic vegetables. The salt also helps them expel some water when they're cooking.

3. Now put the mushrooms on top of the carrots and the potato cubes on top of those.

4. Put another sprinkling of salt and pepper on top. You need to make sure everything is very well seasoned; otherwise your packet will be bland. You can use any sort of sauces you want to put on top.

5. Drizzle everything with a good dose of olive oil, a tablespoon or two. Next shake on some soy sauce. Just a teaspoon or so. Then, pour on 2 to 3 tablespoons of the barbecue sauce. Lastly, add some hot sauce if you'd like to give it a kick

6. Seal it up.

7. Next, you need to seal the packet really, really well. If your packet is already on a cookie sheet like I advised, great! If not, put it on one. Then stick it in your preheated oven. Bake for 1 hour.

8. When your hobo packet comes out of the oven, let it sit and cool for at least five to ten minutes. Then put it on a plate and carefully open it up. There's a lot of steam in there. Make a little bowl out of your aluminum foil and eat.

FOIL WRAPPED VEGGIES

INGREDIENTS:

- 2 1/2 pounds new potatoes, thinly sliced
- 1 large sweet potato, thinly sliced
- 2 onions, sliced 1/4 inch thick
- 1/2 pound fresh green beans, cut into 1 inch pieces
- 1 sprig fresh rosemary
- 1 sprig fresh thyme
- 2 tablespoons olive oil
- salt and pepper to taste
- 1/4 cup olive oil

METHOD:

1. Preheat grill for high heat.
2. In a large bowl, combine the new potatoes, sweet potato, onions, green beans, rosemary, and thyme. Stir in 2 tablespoons olive oil, salt, and pepper to coat.
3. Using 2 to 3 layers of foil, create desired number of foil packets. Brush inside surfaces of packets liberally with remaining olive oil. Distribute vegetable mixture evenly among the packets. Seal tightly.
4. Place packets on the preheated grill. Cook 30 minutes, turning once, or until potatoes are tender.

GRILLED VEGETABLES IN FOIL PACKETS

INGREDIENTS:

- 1/2 cup canola oil

- 1/4 cup cider vinegar

- clove garlic, minced

- 1 tsp sea salt

- 1/2 tsp pepper

- 1/2 pound green beans, trimmed

- 1/2 pound yellow wax beans, trimmed

- red bell pepper, seeded, cut into 1/2-inch strips

- yellow bell pepper, seeded, cut into 1/2-inch strips

- zucchini, trimmed, cut into 1/4-inch rounds

- summer squash, trimmed, cut into 1/4-inch rounds

METHOD:

1. Preheat grill to medium. Cut 6 12-by-18-inch pieces of heavy-duty foil.

2. In a large bowl, whisk oil, vinegar, garlic, seasoned salt and pepper. Add vegetables; toss to coat. Divide vegetables evenly among foil pieces. Drizzle with any remaining dressing.

3. Fold long sides of foil toward each other, crimping edges to seal. Fold and crimp remaining edges, forming a sealed packet.

4. Place packets, seam side up, on grill. Close grill and cook for 20 minutes. To check for doneness, remove one packet from grill, open carefully and taste a vegetable: It should be crisp-tender. Carefully open packets and serve.

FOIL-PACK VEGETABLES

INGREDIENTS:

- 1 cup Button mushrooms

- 1 cup Cherry tomatoes, large

- 1 Zucchini, cut into 1-1/2 inch chunks

- 1/4 cup Kraft zesty Italian dressing, Lite

- 1 Pepper, cut into 1-1/2 inch pieces, red and yellow

METHOD:

1. Ripe veggies steam in their own juices and zesty dressing in a no-mess foil pack.

GRILLED TOFU AND VEGETABLE

INGREDIENTS:

- 1 (10-oz.) pkg. firm or extra-firm tofu, well drained, cut into 8 cubes 1 cup fresh or canned pineapple chunks

- 1medium zucchini, cut into 1/2-inch-thick slices

- 1small yellow summer squash, cut into 1/2-inch-thick slices

- 1red bell pepper, cut into 16 pieces

- 1/4 cup purchased jerk seasoning sauce

METHOD:

2. Heat grill. Cut four 18x12-inch pieces of heavy-duty foil; spray with nonstick cooking spray.

3. In medium bowl, combine all ingredients except seasoning sauce. Drizzle with sauce; toss gently to coat.

4. Divide mixture evenly onto sprayed foil pieces. Wrap each packet securely using double-fold seals, allowing room for heat expansion.

5. When ready to grill, place packets on grill over medium heat or

6. Cook 15 to 20 minutes or until vegetables are tender, turning packets over once.

7. Open packets carefully to allow steam to escape.

TERIYAKI SUMMER VEGETABLE FOIL PACKS

INGREDIENTS:

- 2 cups fresh baby carrots

- 2 cups Green Giant™ SELECT® frozen sugar snap peas

- 1red bell pepper, cut into 8 lengthwise wedges

- 1/4 cup purchased teriyaki baste and glaze

- 1/8 teaspoon ginger

- 1/4 cup chopped fresh cilantro

METHOD:

1. Heat grill. Cut four 18x12-inch pieces of foil. Place carrots, sugar snap peas and bell pepper in center of each piece of foil.

2. In small bowl, combine teriyaki baste and glaze and ginger; mix well. Drizzle mixture over vegetables. Wrap each packet securely using double-fold seals, allowing room for heat expansion.

3. When ready to grill, place packets, seam side up, on grill over medium heat Cook 15 to 20 minutes or until vegetables are crisp-tender.

4. To serve, open packets carefully to allow steam to escape. Sprinkle each with cilantro.

GRILLED VEGETABLE FOIL PACK

INGREDIENTS:

- 2 ears fresh sweet corn, husks removed, each cut into 4 pieces

- 4 small (new) red potatoes (about 1/2 lb.), each cut in half

- 2 carrots cut diagonally into 1 to 1 1/4-inch chunks

- 1medium zucchini, cut into 1-inch chunks

- 1medium onion, cut into thin wedges

- 1/4 cup coconut oil

- 2 tablespoons Dijon mustard

- 1/2 teaspoon dried thyme leaves

- 1/4 teaspoon salt

- 1/4 teaspoon pepper

METHOD:

1. Heat grill. In large bowl, combine corn, potatoes, carrots, zucchini and onion.

2. In small bowl, combine all remaining ingredients; mix well.

3. Pour coconut oil mixture over vegetables; toss to coat.

4. Cut four 18x12-inch pieces of heavy-duty foil. Wrap each packet securely using double-fold seals, allowing room for heat expansion.

5. When ready to grill, place packets, seam side up, on grill over medium heat or on charcoal grill 4 to 6 inches from medium coals.

6. Cook 25 to 35 minutes or until vegetables are tender.

7. To serve, open packets carefully to allow steam to escape.

AROMATIC TOFU PACKETS

INGREDIENTS:

- 1 1/4 pounds firm or extra-firm tofu

- 1/4 cup soy sauce (use a wheat-free version for gluten-free)

- 1 tablespoon mirin

- 1 teaspoon vegetable broth powder (gluten-free if needed; optional)

- 1/4 cup water

- 1-inch piece fresh ginger, peeled and grated

- 1 stalk lemongrass, trimmed, pounded, and minced

- 2 jalapeño or other chili peppers seeded and thinly sliced

- 2 scallions, white and light green parts only, thinly sliced lengthwise

- Half an orange or yellow bell pepper, finely diced

- Freshly ground black pepper

- 2 pieces long pepper, crushed in a mortar and pestle

- 1 lime, cut into wedges

METHOD:

1. Preheat the oven to 400°F.

2. If using banana leaves, you must make them pliable first. Cut out any thick ribs and either boil them for 20 minutes or use tongs to run them over a hot flame.

3. Cut the tofu into 8 evenly sized slabs about 1/2 inch thick. Holding your knife at an angle to the surface of your cutting board, score each slice in two perpendicular directions, being careful not to cut all the way through, with cuts about 1/4 inch apart.

4. Combine the soy sauce, mirin, broth powder and water. Place two pieces of tofu in the center of each piece of parchment paper or banana leaf, and spoon a tablespoon or two of the sauce over each one.

5. Evenly divide the ginger, lemongrass, jalapeño pepper, scallions, and bell pepper among the packets. Season each with several grinds of black pepper and a big pinch of long pepper.

6. Fold the top half of the parchment paper or banana leaf down over the tofu, then fold the bottom half up over the top; crimp the top and bottom halves together.

7. Fold the open sides under twice to make a firm seal, moderately tight around the ingredients, but leave a bit of room for steam. Secure the sides with toothpicks.

8. Place the packets on a baking sheet and bake for 20 minutes.

9. To serve, place each packet on an individual plate. Tell the diners to open them carefully and enjoy the aromatic steam. Pass the lime wedges.

Roasted Portobello Mushroom Packets with Garlic, Shallots, and Balsamic Vinegar

Ingredients:

- 5 large Portobello mushrooms, tops wiped clean and stems and gills removed

- 2 medium shallots, coarsely chopped

- 10-15 cloves of garlic, pre-peeled (go buy it at Costco!)

- Macadamia nut oil, avocado oil, lard, or ghee

- Balsamic Vinegar (I use Trader Joe's Gold Quality Balsamic Vinegar of Modena)

- Salt and Freshly Ground Black Pepper

- 5 large pieces of heavy duty aluminum foil (your mushrooms can burn if you use regular aluminum foil)

Method:

1. Preheat oven to 400 F and coarsely chop the shallots and trim the ends of the garlic

2. Throw the shallots and garlic into food processor or finely mince by hand

3. Add your choice of fat and vinegar to the minced alliums in a 3:1 ratio of oil to vinegar. Season the vinaigrette

mixture with a good sprinkling of salt and freshly ground black pepper

4. Place each Portobello mushroom on a piece of foil, stem side up.

5. Lightly coat each mushroom with extra virgin olive oil and some salt and pepper.

6. Put a dollop of vinaigrette into each mushroom, spreading until the cap is filled.

7. Tightly seal each mushroom packet and place on a baking tray. Stick the tray in the oven and roast for ~25 minutes.

8. Remove mushroom from packets (watch out for steam!) and slice up.

RICE, TOFU AND VEGETABLE PACKETS

INGREDIENTS:

- 1cup cooked short-grain brown or basmati rice
- (1/2-inch-thick) slice firm tofu cut lengthwise across the 1 pound block
- 2large mushrooms, thinly sliced
- 2 thin slices Spanish or red onion
- 2 red bell pepper rings
- 1/4cup shredded carrots
- 1tablespoon low-sodium soy sauce or tamari
- 2tablespoons shredded mozzarella cheese
- 1/2teaspoon dried oregano

METHOD:

1. Preheat oven to 375F.Place a 12-inch-long piece of foil in front of you on work surface.

2. Place rice in center of foil. Top with tofu, then spread vegetables over tofu in a neat pile. Sprinkle with soy sauce, cheese and oregano.

3. Bring edges of foil up around filling and double-fold seams to seal or twist all edges. Place on a baking pan and bake 30 minutes until heated through. Carefully open package to allow steam to escape.

GRILLED CHEESY POTATO PACK

INGREDIENTS:

- 4 cups frozen potatoes with onions and peppers (from 24-oz bag)

- 1 tablespoon vegetable oil

- 1/2 teaspoon seasoned salt

- 3/4 cup shredded smoked tofu cheese

METHOD:

1. Heat grill and spray 1 (18x13-inch) sheet of heavy-duty foil with cooking spray.

2. Place potatoes on center of foil. Drizzle with oil; sprinkle with seasoned salt.

3. Bring up 2 sides of foil over potatoes so edges meet. Seal edges, making tight 1/2-inch fold; fold again, allowing space for heat circulation and expansion. Fold other sides to seal.

4. Place packet on grill over medium heat. Cover grill; cook 30 minutes, turning once.

5. Carefully open packet; sprinkle tofu cheese over potatoes.

6. Cover loosely; let stand 4 to 5 minutes.

GRILLED POTATOES AND ONIONS

INGREDIENTS:

- 12 oz. scrubbed new potatoes, diced into 1/2 inch cubes

- 1 c. chopped onion

- 2 tbsp. chopped fresh parsley (or 2 tsp. dried)

- 1/2 tsp. salt

- 1 1/2 tbsp. coconut oil

METHOD:

1. Get 20 x 12 inch piece heavy - duty aluminum foil.

2. Combine ingredients, with coconut oil on top.

3. Fold foil over potatoes and securely seal ends to make packet.

4. Grill potato packet 30 to 35 minutes or until tender.

GRILLED FRENCH FRIES

INGREDIENTS:

- 1bag of frozen French fries
- 1/4 to 1/2 tsp. dried dill
- 2 to 3 tbsp. creamy Italian dressing
- 1 to 2 tbsp. minced onion
- 1/2 c. grated tofu cheese

METHOD:

1. In large bowl, mix all ingredients (except tofu cheese) and put in a double foil packet, sealing edges tightly.

2. Grill over hot coals for 10 to 15 minutes.

3. Turn packet over and punch holes in foil to vent steam.

4. Grill 10 to 15 minutes more.

5. Open packet carefully because of steam, place French fried in a warmed serving dish and toss with 1/2 cup of grated tofucheese.

GRILLED EGGPLANT AND TOMATO

INGREDIENTS:

- 1/2-2/3 c. chopped fresh basil leaves
- 4-5 tbsp. olive oil
- 2 cloves garlic, crushed
- 1tsp. salt
- 1tsp. freshly ground black pepper
- 1 lg. eggplant, about 1 1/2 lb. each
- 4 sm. fresh ripe tomatoes (1 lb.)
- Fresh basil sprigs, optional
- Foil for wrapping

METHOD:

1. In small bowl, mix basil, oil, garlic, salt and pepper.
2. Cut each eggplant into about 10 thin lengthwise slices, starting at bottom and leaving top intact.
3. Place each eggplant on doubled 14 x 12 inch sheet of foil.
4. Brush slices on both sides with basil-oil mixture. Separating eggplant slices to make a fan inserted 2 or 3 slices between each.

5. Cover each eggplant with second double sheet of foil, crimp top and bottom edges to seal tightly.

6. When coals are ready, place foil packets on grill, cook with grill covered about 30 minutes until eggplant is tender.

7. Remove tops of packets carefully.

8. Drizzle eggplants with additional oil and chopped basil, is desired and fresh basil sprigs.

CORN ON THE COB

INGREDIENTS:

- 4 ears of shucked corn

- ¼ cup olive oil

- tofu cheese

- ½ teaspoon dried rosemary leaves

- salt and pepper

- 4 ice cubes

METHOD:

1. Place the ears of corn on a large sheet of foil.

2. Spread the olive oil on top.

3. Sprinkle with the seasonings and tofu cheese.

4. Put the ice cubes on top.

5. Wrap up into a tent pack.

6. Place on hot coals and cook for 20 minutes.

GRILLED POTATOES AND ONIONS

INGREDIENTS:

- 12 oz. new potatoes, scrubbed & cubed
- 1 c. chopped onion
- 2 tsp. parsley flakes
- 1/2 tsp. salt
- 1 tbsp. plus 1 tsp. coconut oil

METHOD:

1. Place grill rack 5 inches from coals.
2. On 20 x 12 inch piece of heavy duty aluminum foil combine potatoes, onions, parsley and salt; dot with coconut oil.
3. Fold foil over potatoes, securely seal ends to make a packet.
4. Grill potato packet 30-35 minutes or until tender.

ALL - IN - ONE DINNER PACKET

INGREDIENTS:

- 2 lbs. smoked seitan, steak, cut into 4 pieces

- 4 scallion onions (tops included), chopped

- 4 pieces foil

- 4 med. potatoes, sliced thin

- 4 med. carrots, sliced thin

- 1can vegan gravy

- 1/2 tsp. dill weed

METHOD:

1. On each piece of foil, place 1 slice of seitan and top with sliced potatoes, carrots, and onions.

2. Mix vegan gravy and dill weed together.

3. Spoon over each packet. Seal. Place setan side down on cookie sheet and bake at 350 degrees for 30-40 minutes or until vegetables are tender.

VEGETABLE PACKET

INGREDIENTS:

- 1/2 teaspoon Black pepper, freshly ground
- 3/4 teaspoon cumin
- 1/4 teaspoon paprika
- 1 tablespoon dried oregano
- 1 1/2 teaspoons olive oil or canola oil
- 2 tablespoons Chopped fresh chives
- 1 lemon, thinly sliced
- 4 teaspoons caper, drained
- 1 cup sugar snaps peas
- 1 cup cut fresh carrots
- 2 tomatoes, sliced
- 1 fennel bulb, thinly sliced

METHOD:

1. Preheat grill to medium-high. In a small bowl, mix together pepper, cumin, paprika, and oregano.

2. Season vegetables with combined spices.

3. Cut eight 20-inch-long pieces of foil. Layer two sheets for each packet

4. Arrange each portion on one half of each double layer.

5. Top all with chives, 1 or 2 lemon slices, capers, snap peas, carrots, tomatoes, and fennel.

6. Fold the foil over the ingredients and tightly seal the packets by crimping and folding edges together.

7. Grill for 10 to 12 minutes, rotating the packets 180 degrees about halfway through to ensure even cooking.

8. Let packets rest unopened for 5 minutes before serving.

9. Instruct diners to open the sealed side of the packet away from them, as the escaping steam is hot.

GRILLED MUSHROOMS IN FOIL PACKETS

INGREDIENTS:

- 1pound large regular, Portobello mushrooms, cleaned, trimmed and sliced 1/2 inch thick

- 2 tablespoons chopped fresh thyme, mint, sage, rosemary or marjoram

- 2 to 4 garlic cloves, thinly sliced or chopped

- Salt

- freshly ground pepper to taste

- 2 tablespoons extra virgin olive oil, plus additional for brushing foil

METHOD:

1. Cut four 12-by-12-inch squares of heavy aluminum foil, or eight squares of regular aluminum foil

2. In a large bowl, combine the mushrooms, herbs, garlic, salt and pepper, and olive oil. Use a large spoon to blend the ingredients.

3. Brush the dull side of the aluminum squares with olive oil, and divide the mushrooms among the four squares.

4. Fold the squares over and crimp the edges together to form well-sealed packets. Place on a hot grill, and grill 20 to 25 minutes.

5. Remove one packet from the grill, and place on a plate.

6. Carefully open it to check for doneness. The mushrooms should be tender and juicy.

7. Either transfer to plates or bowls (there will be lots of juice), or cut the packets and eat the mushrooms directly from them.

SPICY OLIVES

INGREDIENTS:

- 1cup olives
- 1/2 teaspoon red pepper flakes
- 1minced garlic clove

METHOD:

1. Toss 1 cup olives, 1/2 teaspoon red pepper flakes and 1 minced garlic clove on a sheet of foil.
2. Form a packet.
3. Grill over medium-high heat, turning often, 15 minutes.

POPCORN

INGREDIENTS:

- 1 tablespoon vegetable oil

- 1/4 cup popcorn kernels

- Salt to taste

METHOD:

1. Combine 1 tablespoon vegetable oil and 1/4 cup popcorn kernels in a disposable pie pan.

2. Seal the pan in foil, making a dome shape on top. (Use 2 sheets of foil, if needed, to cover.)

3. Grill over high heat, shaking, until the popping stops, about 8 minutes.

4. Season with salt.

SOUTHWESTERN POTATO PACKET

INGREDIENTS:

- 1onion, thinly sliced

- 1-1/2 lb. potatoes (about 4), cut into 1/2-inch cubes

- 1/4 tsp. chili powder

- 1/4 tsp. ground cumin

- 1can (4-1/2 oz.) chopped green chilies, undrained

- 1cup Shredded spicy tofu Cheese

- 1/2 cup TACO BELL® Thick & Chunky Salsa

- 1/2 cup yogurt

- 1/4 cup chopped fresh cilantro

METHOD:

1. Heat grill to medium-high heat.

2. Spray large sheet of heavy-duty foil with cooking spray.

3. Place onions in center of foil; top with potatoes. Mix chili powder and cumin; sprinkle over potatoes. Top with chilies.

4. Fold foil to make packet.

5. Grill 30 min. or until potatoes are tender.

6. Cut slits in foil to release steam before carefully opening packet.

7. Sprinkle with tofu cheese.

8. Let stand 2 min.

9. Serve topped with salsa, yogurt and cilantro.

Peperoni Spiced Seitan

Ingredients:

- 11/2 cups vital wheat gluten
- 1/4 cup nutritional yeast
- 1 tsp salt
- 2 tsp paprika
- 1 tsp cayenne
- 1/2 tsp ground fennel
- 1/8 tsp allspice
- 1/2 cup + 2 tbsp. water
- 2 tbsp. red wine
- 4 tbsp. tomato paste
- 2 tbsp. olive oil
- 2 tbsp. vegan Worcestershire sauce

Method:

1. Mix dry ingredients together in a bowl. Dissolve tomato paste in the water and wine. Mix all liquid ingredients into the dry ingredients.
2. Combine thoroughly. Knead several times.

3. Roll into a log shape about 2 inches in diameter. Lightly spray a piece of foil with cooking spray.

4. Wrap the seitan dough in the foil, making sure to wrap the foil around in the log completely at least twice to keep it under wraps while it bakes.

5. Put on a baking sheet and bake at 325F for 90 minutes, rolling the log once during baking so the top and the bottom both get time on the baking sheet.

6. Cool completely in the foil, then freeze or fridge as desired.

Seitan Roast

Ingredients:

- 2 cups vital wheat gluten
- 2 Tbsp. unbleached all-purpose flour
- 1/4 cup nutritional yeast
- 1 tsp. garlic powder
- 1 tsp. onion powder
- 1 tsp. dried sage
- 1 tsp. Italian seasoning
- 1 1/2 cups cold water
- 1/2 cup low-sodium soy sauce
- 2 Tbsp. tomato paste
- 1 Tbsp. extra virgin olive oil

Method:

1. Combine all of the dry ingredients in a large bowl. Mix all of the wet ingredients in a large measuring cup.

2. Pour the wet ingredients into the dry ingredients and mix with a wooden spoon until it creates a dough.

3. Use your hands to knead the dough (either in the bowl or on a large cutting board) for 3 minutes. This will develop

the elasticity of the dough. If the dough is too wet, add a little bit more vital wheat gluten. If the dough is too dry, add a little more water. Let rest for 10 minutes after kneading.

4. Meanwhile, preheat oven to 350 degrees F and prepare baking sheet.

5. Lay two sheets of aluminum foil of equal length, as long as your baking sheet, onto the pan, overlapping each other lengthwise by 6 inches. Lay a sheet of parchment paper over the center of the aluminum foil.

6. Knead the dough one last time for 30 seconds, then form into a log shape. Place log over the parchment paper

7. Wrap the log first with the parchment paper, then with the aluminum foil, folding it over the top.

8. Roll in the edges of the aluminum foil to make a sealed packet. It should be sealed well, but not too tight - it will need a little bit of room to expand.

9. Bake in the oven for 1 hour, pausing to flip the packet every 15 minutes to ensure even cooking (wide tongs work well for this). Remove from oven, carefully open packet, and serve seitan as desired.

GRILLED POTATO AND ASPARAGUS FOIL PACK

INGREDIENTS:

- 1cup small potatoes
- 1/2 cup chopped fresh asparagus spears
- 1/4 cup diagonally sliced green onions (4 medium)
- 1teaspoons grape seed oil
- 1/2 teaspoon salt
- 1/4 teaspoon pepper

METHOD:

1. Heat gas or charcoal grill. Tear off 12-inch length of heavy-duty foil to make packet. Lightly spray 1 side of foil (side that will be inside of packet) with canola oil cooking spray.

2. Place potatoes in 2-quart saucepan; cover potatoes with water. Heat to boiling. Reduce heat; cook until potatoes are just tender, about 10 minutes. Drain potatoes; return to saucepan. Add remaining ingredients; toss gently.

3. Place mixture in center of foil. Bring up 2 sides of foil so edges meet. Seal edges, making tight 1/2-inch fold; fold again, allowing space on sides for heat circulation and expansion. Fold other sides to seal.

4. Place foil packet on grill. Cover grill; cook 12 to 15 minutes, turning packet once. Cooking times are approximate and depend on the heat of your grill.

FOIL-PACK BROCCOLI

INGREDIENTS:

- 1bag (12 oz) Green Giant™ Steamers™ Select™ frozen broccoli florets

- 1tablespoon lemon juice

- 1 tablespoon olive oil

- 1/2 teaspoon salt

- 1/4 teaspoon pepper

- 3 tablespoons shredded tofu cheese

METHOD:

1. Heat gas or charcoal grill to medium-high heat. Tear off 2 (12-inch) lengths heavy-duty foil to make foil packets.

2. Place half the broccoli in center of each piece of foil. Drizzle with lemon juice, olive oil and salt.

3. Bring up 2 sides of foil so edges meet. Seal edges, making tight 1/2-inch fold.

4. Fold again, allowing space on sides for heat circulation and expansion. Fold other sides to seal.

5. Place foil packets on grill over indirect heat. Cover grill; cook 15 to 25 minutes or until broccoli is heated through. Carefully open foil packs, and sprinkle broccoli with tofu cheese.

6. Serve immediately.

ROASTED VEGETABLE PACKETS

INGREDIENTS:

- 1recipe pepperoni-spiced seitan or 1 lb. kielbasa, cut into 1/2" slices or chunks

- 1 eggplant or 2 medium zucchini, cut into 1" cubes

- 2 bell peppers, cut into 1" pieces

- 1 lb. small potatoes, halved

- olive oil

METHOD:

1. Place potatoes in a microwave-safe bowl and nuke 3-4 minutes to precook.

2. Evenly divide all ingredients among 6 large foil squares.

3. Drizzle with olive oil and fold up tightly to seal.

4. Fridge now if desired for same-day or next-day cooking.

5. Bake packets 30 minutes at 400F or grill them about 30 minutes.

Muffins in an Orange Shell

Ingredients:

- 6 oranges

- 1package of just-add-water muffin mix

Method:

1. Mix up the muffin mix as instructed.

2. Cut off the quarter top of the oranges.

3. Carefully scoop out the pulp; do not break the skin.

4. Pour the muffin mix into the oranges.

5. Wrap the oranges in foil, crimping the foil around the hole at top of the shell, but leaving it open.

6. Place the oranges upright in a stable position on hot coals and cook for about 10-15 minutes.

PINEAPPLE DONUT CAKE

INGREDIENTS:

- 1 ring of pineapple

- 1 tablespoon coconut oil

- 1 tablespoon brown sugar

- 1 cake donut

METHOD:

1. Place donut on sheet of foil.

2. Mix the coconut oil and brown sugar together and spread it over the donut.

3. Place the pineapple ring on top.

4. Wrap the donut in a tight flat pack.

5. Place on hot coals and cook for 5-7 minutes.

APPLES IN FOIL PACKET

INGREDIENTS:

- 1Granny Smith apple, cored
- 1 tablespoon brown sugar
- 1/4 teaspoon ground cinnamon

METHOD:

1. Fill the core of the apple with the brown sugar and cinnamon.

2. Wrap the apple in a large piece of heavy foil, twisting the extra foil into a tail for a handle.

3. Place the apple in the coals of a campfire or barbeque and let cook 5 to 10 minutes, until softened.

4. Remove and unwrap, being careful of the hot sugar.

CONCLUSION

I made many efforts for many years to spread the message of optimal nutrition for each and every one of us in a clear and easy way to understand, even for beginners.

Given the success of my healthy cooking courses, I decided to bring this welcome trend to the attention of as many people as I can around the world.

The whole humanity deserves to learn how to live correctly in terms of diet and lifestyle in general.

I thank you, dear readers for the interest in this booklet and I highly recommend reviewing our long line of booklets, that comes to teach us how to live in a healthy way, improving our living habits and how to raise our children in the best possible manner.

1.

Made in the USA
San Bernardino, CA
16 October 2018